This collection shapes itself [...] that *nothing of beauty is ever u[...]* a needed one—in times like ours. These poems are grounded in the long remembering of loss and shaped by the tender work of grief. They are brimming with epiphanies-in-the-ordinary, which after all, are the only ones that startle us into seeing our own lives anew. Here, you'll find poems of generous remembering, offering subterranean glimpses into those tender shoots of loss that go deep as they spread down through the years and ground us in gratitude. They'll remind you, in their freshness, of what poetry is for, inviting you to indwell your own life with greater attentiveness and learn to see what is familiar with an unexpected generosity of feeling. In reading them, you'll find yourself beckoned to *grow yourself deeper, / to know yourself further in the light.* What more could one hope for in poems—and in life?

MARK S. BURROWS
author of *The Chance of Home: Poems* (2018) and,
with Jon M. Sweeney, *Meister Eckhart's Book of Secrets* (2019), and
poetry editor for *Spiritus* and *ARTS*

Andrea Potos is smitten by literature, smitten by life itself. Her fine lyric poetry converses with great voices from the past, including Dickinson, Alcott, Keats, the Brontes, and Dorothy Wordsworth. *Her Joy Becomes* is a book for those of us who find our prayers in poems, who find greatest joy in daily life with loved ones, books, the natural world, observing miracles occurring before our eyes. From "Poets": *while inspiration garbed itself / in the bodies of birds / and invisible molecules of ordinary air.* *Her Joy Becomes* is a book to carry in purse or backpack for solace on the go.

DONNA HILBERT
author of *Threnody,*
and *Gravity: New & Selected Poems*

Open *Her Joy Becomes*, and *your heart / will tap Yes*. These vivid, beautifully observed pieces immerse us in a time *when the thin air / between worlds was still / noticeable and ordinary*. Don't miss this collection. Andrea Potos's poems call us to fully inhabit our lives as the best poetry always does.

LAURA GRACE WELDON
author of *Portals*,
2019 Ohio Poet of the Year

These poems are openings to wonder, traversing the seasons of the year and of the heart. Andrea Potos invites us into the intimacy of the color and texture of life. From journeying with her mother through illness to observations of the writer's call, this collection feels filled with the possible. As the reader, I feel enlarged.

CHRISTINE VALTERS PAINTNER
author of *Dreaming of Stones*
and *The Wisdom of Wild Grace*

Her Joy Becomes

Poems by Andrea Potos

Fernwood
PRESS

Her Joy Becomes

©2022 by Andrea Potos

Fernwood Press
Newberg, Oregon
www.fernwoodpress.com

Printed in the United States of America

Cover and page design: Mareesa Fawver Moss
Cover photo: Freddie Addery
Author photo: Katrin Talbot

ISBN 978-1-59498-024-4

For all the marigold days

Table of Contents

Joy is the serious business of Heaven.
—C.S. Lewis

*What did you think, that joy
was some slight thing?*
—Mark Doty

Surely joy is the condition of life.
—Henry David Thoreau

Gathering

As you begin, look just slant,
the same way one should not look directly
into the sun's gaze.
Graze with your consciousness,
keeping your hands nimble, your reach a fluency
of light as words begin to sift
and fall and settle where they
know they belong.

Part One

Part One

Abundance to Share with the Birds

Another early morning
in front of the bathroom mirror—
my daughter making faces
at herself while I pull
back her long brown hair,
gathering the breadth and shine
in my hands, brushing
and smoothing before weaving
the braid she will wear
to school for the day.
Afterward, stray strands
nestle in the brush, and because
nothing of beauty is ever wasted,
I pull them out,
stand on the porch and let them fly.

Late Autumn Crochet

When asked again, I have to explain
I'm not *making* anything.
I am practicing unfurling
tangled skeins of incessant thought
along these lengthening rows of double-stitch crochet
my Yaya taught me forty years ago—shining
copper hook in my right hand, and on my lap,
russet gold and dark teal, sage green and burgundy—
gathered emblems of the season, what I need for bracing
against the bitterness to come, a semblance of pattern
for discarding shreds of worry, wrapping the hours
in some fashion of blessing and warmth.

Trying to Teach My Mother to Crochet

I wanted something for her hands—
the dusky blue crochet hook I bought for her
and blue acrylic yarn the color
of the Greek sea near the long-ago
city of her birth.

She didn't ask for this lesson.
In her steady kindness, she went along
with me, trying to match her fingers
to the flow of looping yarn.
I worried she wouldn't continue
when her mind told her
she needed another cigarette,

though the cancer had already set in both lungs
and her treatment begun. I never considered
how she might want to live her last months or years
doing what gave her balm, the familiar comfort
to inhale, taste and release a swirling elegance
of smoke. All I knew was my own need
to halt what had already begun, to keep her
present and seamlessly shawled around us.

In the Imaging Room

The lights were dim, a gray screen
lit with numbers I couldn't see from where
I lay. The technician kept her quiet,
would not admit to seeing *anything interesting*
when I asked. *I cannot diagnose.*
I wanted conversational relief
for my pinched discomfort, my breath a stalled
bird kept in my throat, only released when
I turned my gaze to the wall—
a painting of seashells I discerned
enough in the light—pale pink conch
and abalone, moon snail and scallop.
And in the center, a chambered nautilus,
its spiraled heart reaching toward mine.

The Mammogram Technician Asked
if I Wanted to Take a Look

Profile of a motherland—
sloping hill and veins bold
with blood ore,
rivers of light criss-
crossing and coursing
from view, I prayed
my eyes were true—
I saw no errant stone.

Sleep Skills

These days I wake up tired
after hours skimming sleep's
surface like a hungry bird, waiting.
They say it's a fact of growing older,
to lose the skill for sleep infants
and teenagers mindlessly have.

I think of my Yaya; when I was a girl,
she was already dressed before first light,
her body telling her it was time
to live the day, tend to her needles and thread,
her yarn. And in her kitchen, the flour and water
in their porcelain bowls; a woman waiting for the morning
to rise under her hands.

In the Healer's Room

I felt myself carried
across wine-dark waters
as if a ship's manifest were kept
near me, the unknown
and the known—
paternal grandmother Helen,
a scared girl of seven coming over
from Patras;
maternal grandmother Aristea,
an astonished bride of nineteen
from Piraeus, holding my
eight-month-old mother in her arms
as the ship rose and dipped, glided
and churned along the endless
waves for weeks.
I give thanks to the waters
that held them up to land them here,
where I may remember something
of their stories within
my body now.

Remembering Easters in Childhood

Besides my Yaya's juicy lamb and potatoes,
her round, gold bread planted with
a blood-red egg in its center,

it was the clothes I got to wear
that felt like dress-up time:
white patent-leather Mary Janes
newly risen from shoeboxes,
pastel dresses with layers that made me
want to twirl like the ballerina
on top of my jewelry box
and a shiny white barrette
for my hair finally outgrowing its pixie cut.

My mind still takes photographs
of me standing beside my sister and our cousins
on our Yaya's front lawn in the late 52nd Street air,
when the newly strengthened sun still gleamed
above the peaked roofs of the neighborhood.

Say Autumn/For My Mother

after Stanley Plumly

I would give it back to you, perhaps in a season,
say autumn. I would give you back leaves,
ocher, crimson, fire orange of the sprawling maple
across the street from your house, that cherished sight
every October, the month of your birth, midway through
the season, Mother, months of irrepressible beauty and change
deepening. I would give you back more autumns
free from back pain and money worries, still breathing,
no lesions in your lungs. I would give you back my presence
nourished beside you, both of us at your window, rapt,
witness to the daily gift of that October tree.

Crocheting in December

We live to learn new ways to hold
summer sun through winter cold.
　　　—Robert Francis

I'm wandering the craft store aisles—
yarn bins to the ceiling of *blackberry dusk,*
lime sherbet, heather bloom,
grape gala and so much more.
I pass them all to find
what will carry me through
the cruel months to come: the softest acrylic
sunny day—a slight sheen on its surface,
as if dusted with air of high June.

I fill my arms with skeins.
I will take them home, use what I need
for the warmth of winter gold.

Funeral

for my uncle

Twenty-two years his junior,
she was never supposed to leave
him first. I slipped beside him,
wrapped my arm around his shoulder,
felt the dark wool of his suit,
so stately in his sorrow.
Thank you, honey,
he whispered, staring ahead, heavy
and heavier, thick and immovable
in grief, a quarry of stone
he would chip away at for months
to come, all the years left
of her absence beside him.
We could not yet glimpse
the new form he would become.

Small Ode to Laundry on the Line

Oh to be the washed linens and sheets,

the towels and blouses and trousers,

all the underpinnings of dailiness—all sailing

and flapping on a sturdy line, releasing

their music of fabric to the air—

to be so wind-rinsed and cleansed,

so sun-seeped

down the deepest thread.

On Dreams

They crowd in,
hogging all the room in my sleep,
not life altering or Technicolor
like you read about in inspirational memoirs—
more like busted puzzle pieces
or wrappers tossed from open car windows
to flitter across the roads
or jumble sales in church basements,
where it is upstairs that Light
burns through the magnificent windows.

Sometimes, I Notice

I may have become
my mother—wearing a soft
plaid blouse she would wear,
my mouth turning its corners into a smile
at small delights:
relief of the heating pad
on my spasmed back muscle,
a plate of homemade ravioli
from my neighbor two doors down.

How to explain the wholeness
I inhabit, as if I have learned how to abide
with her lost physical form,
and she and I are together, both of us
giggling, a sound suddenly
like the tinkling of ice cubes
in the tall glass of soda she enjoyed each night.

Her Decision

This time it came not from
some sprung blaze of the instant.

It arrived more
as an ocher mellowing,
a ripening
in some untended field.

A peace whispered to her,
Step away,
a different happiness unfolding.

Mom, Now

after Robert Francis

Residing in all the rooms
of thought, around
my heart she keeps
shelter and lamp,

air of balm and solace
of being, endurance
of her embrace,
unseen.

Spots of Time

with thanks to Annie Lighthart

This could be one—
me wearing seersucker again, fifty years after
I was the child in the playsuit my Yaya
sewed for me—

a coolness embedded in the threads—
breezes of early June mornings,
refreshment of my Yaya's lawn,
its unmown depths and permission.

If this fabric were a plant, it might be
a patch of dew-bright parsley
or mint, picked just now
from her everlasting garden.

Kitchen Magic

While sighing into another shift
at the kitchen sink, so many
plates and pans, all the flatware
I need to keep from falling
into the open disposal,
it appeared—one lone bubble
no bigger than a dime,
iridescent orb floating even with my eye.
I followed its rise like a miniature balloon
from Heaven's fairground; up and to the left
it traveled, into the dining room where
I soon lost its trail, where I did not witness
the transformation into its next
undying form.

Witch of the Morning

To pour
then hear the grinder's
whirl and crunch,
to scatter the dark
scent, bitter
and nut hued,
to bring forth water to bathe
and seep so
grounds become
brew, become
joy, medicine,
ordinary elixir—
earth magic alive
on the mortal tongue.

Ode to the Laura Ashley Shops
of the '70s and '80s

Oh the dream of an hour
stepping across the warm maple floorboard

aisles of blossoming dresses
that were more than dresses—

bestowers of gardens and roses
and sunflowers, they were

trellises and arbors,
meadows and groves of fabric,

hems and sleeves of sunlit grasses,
cotton that gentled the body

into belonging on this earth.

Gratitude in Early June

To wake before the usual hour,
the day so generous to begin,
the morning gentle
to stir you,

to give yourself another hour,
grow yourself deeper,
to know yourself further in the light.

Life List

abridged version

Black coffee and cranberry scones,

inland lakes and ocean waves,

glory months of October and June,

the constant quest for equanimity,

paper and fast-writing pens,

books and more books,

daughter and mother,

husband and friend,

Emily Dickinson's Hope—

what taps my windowsill

holds my gaze, keeps returning

upon my pointed will.

Part Two

Poets

We are busy doing nothing.
    —Billy Collins

I'm busy cherishing the warmth
from my coffee mug this morning,
the one I carried across the ocean
from John Keats's house in London.
My palms cup the words
painted with the opening
draft of his timeless
nightingale ode, words crossed out,
and I can't discern what came before *drowsy*—
My heart aches, and a drowsy numbness pains—
his penmanship is two centuries old
after all; two whole centuries ago he drowsed
for hours on a brilliant May morning
under the plum tree in the front garden,
while inspiration garbed itself
in the bodies of birds
and invisible molecules of ordinary air.

Lost Brontë Library Resurfaces

*Highlights include a handwritten manuscript of Emily Bronte's
poems. . . . It carries an estimate of 1.3 million to 1.8 million.*
—New York Times, May 25, 2021

What would it mean to stand inches
from those fragile pages, ink
from her hand long since sunk
through to the other side—
watermarks to the other world.
Her poems laid open to the auctioneer's table:
*The countless links are strong
That bind us to our clay,*
a roomful of expectant, rising hands
to claim the privilege for themselves or
to offer it elsewhere for all pilgrims to attend:
*Lust of fame was but a dream
That vanished with the morn.*

Brontean Morning

The loudest crows
cawing over the tops of the oaks
call me to autumn already,
and though my back is to the window,

I know the sky must be a gray wuthering,
and the curlews are crying. The wind
must be moaning as it goes sweeping
across heath and moors and the spikes
of purple heather thousands of miles away
from where my body sits; yet

I feel the gorse
grazing my ankles as I go.

On Reading John Donne for the First Time

In the center of my chest, a kindling
there in the hollow,

as if a match had just
been struck, or the blinds
snapped up on a sealed room,

gold suffusing the air, and through
the wide windows, a solstice unfolding,
mine for the lengthening days.

No Touching or Photography Allowed

Orchard House, Concord, Massachusetts

I became the girl wanting only
to breathe the air that carried
the same atoms as their breath,
to see what they daily saw:
Louisa's green mood pillow on the parlor couch,
Marmee's bedroom quilt, the yellowed keys
of sweet Lizzie's melodeon. I wanted to brush my palm
against the breadboard Sister May etched with flames
from the fireplace poker.

In Louisa's bedroom, I stood in the back
while our passionate guide entranced
us with details. I reached
behind me, placed my palm
on the white wooden shelf Bronson cut
and hung off the wall for her:
a half-moon desk
where immortality wrote itself—
I touched it.

Sometimes, in the Silence of the Room

She can feel it like thicknesses
and layers of cloth
or ancestral depths
of something she
will never touch, only know

it is there, bequeathed
to the pure
stillnesses of air,
all the unnamed heartaches,
all the radiant loves.

Before Beginning to Write, I Call Out

Charlotte, Emily, Anne,
incanting their names to the air,

my old sisters, I like to pretend,
considering myself the youngest one

left behind in another century with
fathoms left to learn, my stockinged feet

propped on the fireplace fender as theirs
always were. While they go about their lives now

worlds and worlds ahead of me,
I close my eyes as if

I might inhale even one
waylaid atom of their breath.

Basketball and Poetry

Witness the power forward, who might be mistaken
for a moving skyscraper as he scales the court
in seemingly six steps for the dunk and then the roar.

Witness the poet in her morning hour,
steam from her coffee swirling into her eyes as she hovers
between stillness and form, on the verge of the dive.

Reading an Author's Childhood Memoir,
I Return Briefly to a State of Grace

Those moments when the gates
were not yet latched,
the blinds not yet
drawn down,

when the thin air
between worlds was still
noticeable and ordinary,
brushing the skin from

time to time, though there
was no time,
only now,
the true eternal.

Summer, Childhood

Hours and hours of taffy pulled and stretched
to the furthest reaches of neighborhood lawns, universe
of grasses cool and tickling, cushions
for our bodies somersaulting and cartwheeling, tagging
you're it, while somewhere above us

the dimmer switch of Heaven would be turning
down to lavender rose and deeper rose, and then
the voices of the mothers streaming in
through the darkening air
to *come home, come home.*

Poetry in July

It's one of those rare clear
days, the prickling heat of the last
weeks gone, the blanketed
stodgy haze.
This day could almost be autumn—
lace of coolness in the air, the lake
like beveled cobalt glass.
It's those seasons in between that I love,
without fixed stances of hot
or cold, the way Keats might have
fashioned them: receptive, uncertain,
capable of ardent, bracing imagination.

This Brief Departure from Our Days

Fish Creek, Wisconsin

Four rooms set
on the slope above
the world's commerce.

From inside these borders
of ocher pine
and fireplace as furnace,

a kitchen enough to hold two
and wrought-iron bedsteads with thickly
quilted spreads—

how easy to return
to a time of refuge
when I am not yet born.

To Step Inside the Frame

Renoir's Washerwomen

Oh to be ushered inside
blue and bluer
shallows of the water,
hands swirling the white cloths,
apron grazing the soft banks.
   Oh to kneel at the river's edge,
soak and scrub and rinse, to breathe within
brushstrokes of light.

After Not Being Chosen
to Read at the Emily Dickinson Event

No matter, I remain
nobody
for now,
passed over—

But isn't there still singing from the cherrywood desk?

Days of Dorothy

found poem, Dorothy Wordsworth's journals

Moonshine like herrings in the water.

William went into the woods and altered his poems.

I boiled Coleridge a mutton chop, which he ate in bed.

The quietness and still seclusion of the valley affected me even
to producing the deepest melancholy. I forced myself from it.

Baked bread and giblet pie, a bad giblet pie.

William highly poetical.

All the morning I was busy copying poems.

I was so unlucky as to propose to rewrite "The Pedlar."

The roses in the garden fretted and battered and quite spoiled;
the honeysuckle in its glory is sadly teased.

A very rainy day. I made a shoe.

The leaves drop with the heat of the sun all day long.

Glowworms in abundance.

We walked to the Easedale hills to hunt waterfalls.

The thrush sang all day as he always sings.

William kindled and began the poem.

In woods beyond Gowbarrow Park . . . I never saw daffodils

so beautiful . . . some rested their heads upon the stones as
   on a pillow for weariness.

My tooth broke today. They will soon be gone. Let that pass,
I shall still be beloved, I want no more.

Modern Conversation

I overhear them everywhere—
it's like, and *I'm like*
spilled and smeared into every other
sentence so that I can't help
the urge to wipe up,
toss out, vacuum
speech like some
housekeeper, wordkeeper.
If only this meant they
were on the verge
of similes, drawing closer
to poetry, releasing a grip
on the prosaic and expected,
making each ordinary thing become
something other and something more,
newly conceived, *awesome.*

-7 on a February Morning

In my third-floor garret room, I lie down,
trying to dispel the packed weight
of fatigue in my winter bones.

Then I hear it—through the sealed windows
and pulled shades—lone cardinal, unspooling
pure notes from some stripped, godforsaken tree
out there, perched on some ice-stunned branch—this bird

insistent on joy, reminding me, *yes*,
it will be spring, it will be summer
when I will so easily forget this song.

Time

. . . is eternity living dangerously.
          —John Moriarty

When the moment slips
from itself, flees
the container
of its being,

starts to stride
away, reckless even,
from what could have been
Eden after all.

Interior with a Violin Case

Henri Matisse

Beyond white drapes and French doors,
three blackbirds are on the verge
of flying off a slate-green railing
that hems water and sky.
Blue has ventured within
the room and gathered like deep twilight
inside the violin case spread open
and emptied.
    Somewhere near
there must be music
playing the notes of the sea.

Where I Might Find Her

Overnight it seems, the pink vaults
of the peonies open;
in an iridescent second, a hummingbird
twirls inches from my face.

Pennies spot the sidewalk—so bright
I believe they would smile if they could.

And if kindness were air,
the rooms of my house expand with it.
Breathing deeply is simple, and hope
is the natural choice.

Apple Picking

Winslow Homer

I imagine them sisters
ordered by their mother
to head to the orchard,
gather the ingredients
for this week's pies and staples
to survive the endless
winter ahead.
Their faces are blurred,
their woven baskets tipped to receive.
They stand unmoving, blue
and coral sunbonnets
taken over by light,
as if the sun has finally
claimed its one and true home.

At the Marigold Kitchen Cafe

for Lexi

Its name made good on the promise
of brightness and gold, its burnt orange
and deep ocher walls. We'd find the spot
under the slanted ceiling—our corner
of cushions and embroidered pillows—she
with her sketchbook and magic markers,
her hot cocoa and whipped cream, me
with my wide-ruled notebook and cappuccino; she
drawing stories with her pictures, me learning
by watching how to make pictures with my words.

Late September with Emily

There's a certain slant of light
on autumn afternoons,

a certain sharpness in the air,
as if a heavenly chisel

had carved it clear.
Lapis sky and fields of gold—

all our eyes need know—
an equinox of sight, of soul.

To Jupiter

I don't need a telescope
to know it's you up there
commanding the night
like the Roman god of all gods,
who bears your name. From where I stand,
I can almost see you twinkling
like a giant reddish star, though the books talk
of your hydrogen seas and turbulent, incessant storms,
your vortices of cloud lanes like something from van Gogh,
your unimaginable winds and magnetic tails.

Hard to believe you actually possess no solid surface
anywhere, as I continue to stand, still, out here
in my stockinged feet on a chill October sidewalk,
as if, after all these years, though you are 391 million
miles away from me, I have finally
obeyed your call to stop and see,
to stare as if held, like all of your 63 moons,
by the force of your astonishing gravity.

Small Candle Prayer

for Christine Valters Paintner

Oh to be clothed
in trinities
of light,

an opal set
in the center
of the flame.

Three Acorns from Emily's Yard

I pocketed them that day
the tour guide was not looking.

I nodded to myself that she
would not mind for me to hold

in my palm and carry home
such Possibility.

Poem to the Brussel Sprout

for TJ

Oh much maligned fat-
heads of the garden,
ugly as the Cabbage Patch dolls
of my childhood, for years
I mocked and
avoided you,

then tonight
my brother-in-law, unsung
chef of the family, found you
on sale at Safeway
and brought you home.
He didn't ask us
what we wanted; he
went ahead and let you sizzle
in a silver pan with butter,
pepper, and salt and God knows
what else;
he tossed in a cupful of water
and let you steam,

then heaped you in a blue
porcelain bowl, your bright green
flounces gleaming like petticoats under
the dining room chandelier
while we tasted and tasted
some more. Forgive me
for all those times I have failed
to see beyond a clumsy presence
to the lusciousness of what
is possible and true.

My Father and Pavarotti

On my stereo this morning,
just as I lean in to write, Pavarotti
came on, his aria filling the whole room.
I'm not schooled enough to know
which aria, only how my father loved him
and how, leaving his crabbiness aside, my father
would sit watching the Lake Michigan surf
from his living room window while the great man sang
over the speakers that filled the house;
on the patio of his southern winter home,
he listened, while the lapis surface of the pool sparkled,
then in the last years of the rehab home where he lived
with his rescued brain, a small carved canyon still visible
where the surgeon had rushed in. Once a week I drove
the 80 miles to sit with him there, his silver hair
still blazing, his eyes closed as we absorbed the pure notes
of the rich tenor who sang to my father still.

My Mother Loved Wordsworth

Today I am closing my eyes to bring back
the yellow long-stemmed roses that spilled
over her white coffin,
yellow roses in all of our hands as
the duo of priests chanted in Greek
I did not need to understand.

All I understood was beauty
inscribed on the warm and soft pages
of June air and afternoon echoes
of the poet: *grieve not, rather find*
splendour in the grass,
glory in the flower.

Another Anniversary of My Mother's Passing

Her joy becomes my joy.
    —Rosemerry Wahtola Trommer

This June morning, flickering light and shadow
on the spread pages of my book,
while somewhere above me in the arching
and waving branches of the beeches, one cardinal
keeps throbbing an unceasing song.
And the sky—did I mention the cloudless sky?
The softest blue, as if created
with the pastels of a master, then brushed across
with the gentlest sweep of her arm.

Poets in Eternity

with thanks to Richard Jones

A writer I admire mentioned there being
a desk in a corner of eternity,
and I thought, *yes, that's what*
I want: it doesn't even have to be a traditional
desk with drawers and knobs and things; any
rickety, unvarnished table would do,
even a lap desk, the kind with the cushiony
underside, though I'm pretty sure my sheer
astral form will not need the softness,
only a guarantee that all
that I love to do and praise
will still be mine.

Be Receptive to Signs, She Said

They will not be the bush
ignited as you pass
nor your darkened bedroom lit
by a flock of angels' wings.

What more can I tell you, she said, your heart
will tap *yes* when it comes—
gleaming sidewalk coin of your mother's birth,
dusty scent of your grandmother's jewelry drawer

or essential words you find
in a book your hand opened
like the sea parting its waters.

Another Thing I Miss About Her

is the way she cherished me. And you could say, well,
that is what mothers are supposed to do, isn't it?
And I would say, theoretically yes, but that is not the real
fact of my mother opening her front door and clapping
her hands to see me each Wednesday when I came, nor
is it my mother standing at her big picture window, smiling
with her hand on her chin while she watches
me skip down her front steps, while she waits for me
to unlock my Honda, climb in and snap on my seatbelt,
maybe arrange my soda, my phone and my purse before I start
the engine; all of this and my mother is still visible
through the panes, in no hurry at all while she makes certain
her girl gets off soundly. I can still see her through
the reflected glass, tossing a kiss and waving her soft,
aged hands, *goodbye beautiful and drive safe.*

After the Evening Lecture
on Insight Meditation

I walked under a sky glowing indigo,
past pine trees giving off the last
of their warm scent.
I came home to my husband,
twirled in my long skirt
beside the still-cluttered kitchen sink,
while in the living room our daughter
was up way past bedtime.
I had no urge to scold anyone.
She scurried to her piano;
I heard her hands
release the *Ode to Joy*.

Grateful Acknowledgments

Poetry East:
 "Abundance to Share with the Birds"
 "Gratitude in Early June"
 "Poets"
 "On Reading John Donne for the First Time"
 "Poetry in July"
 "Modern Conversation"

The Sun:
 "Sleep Skills"

Buddhist Poetry Review:
 "Late Autumn Crochet"
 "Reading an Author's Childhood Memoir . . ."
 "This Brief Departure from Our Days"

One Art:
 "Trying to Teach My Mother to Crochet"
 "Sleep Skills"
 "Another Anniversary of My Mother's Passing"
 "My Father and Pavarotti"

Arrows of Light (Iris Press, chapbook):
  "Interior With a Violin Case"
  "The Mammogram Technician Asked . . ."

Braided Way:
  "Say Autumn/For My Mother"

Literary North:
  "Crocheting in December"

Poem:
  "Brontean Morning"

Abundance to Share with the Birds (Finishing Line Press,
  chapbook):
  "Poetry in July"
  "Abundance to Share with the Birds"
  "Modern Conversation"
  "After the Evening Lecture on Insight Meditation"

The Sunlight Press:
  "Where I Might Find Her"

The Path to Kindness: Poems of Connection and Joy (Storey
  Publishing):
  "Where I Might Find Her"
  "Abundance to Share with the Birds"

The Orchards Poetry Journal:
  "Poets in Eternity"

Impspired:
  "Lost Brontë Library Resurfaces"
  "My Mother Loved Wordsworth"
  "Time"

Soul-Lit:
  "Sometimes I Notice"

Loch Raven Review:
 "On Dreams,"
 "No Touching or Photography Allowed,"
 "Basketball and Poetry,"
 "Three Acorns from Emily's Yard"

Title Index

Symbols

A

B

C

First Line Index

CPSIA information can be obtained
at www.ICGtesting.com
Printed in the USA
BVHW082015181022
649509BV00005B/22